1,001 PEARLS OF WISDOM
TO BUILD CONFIDENCE

1,001 PEARLS OF WISDOM TO BUILD CONFIDENCE

Advice and Guidance to Inspire You in Love, Life, and Work

ALAN KEN THOMAS

Skyhorse Publishing

Skyhorse Publishing books may be purchased in bulk at special discounts for sales promotion, corporate gifts, fund-raising, or educational purposes. Special editions can also be created to specifications. For details, contact the Special Sales Department, Skyhorse Publishing, 307 West 36th Street, 11th Floor, New York, NY 10018 or info@skyhorsepublishing.com.

Skyhorse® and Skyhorse Publishing® are registered trademarks of Skyhorse Publishing, Inc.®, a Delaware corporation.

Visit our website at www.skyhorsepublishing.com.

10 9 8 7 6 5 4 3 2 1

Library of Congress Cataloging-in-Publication Data is available on file.

ISBN: 978-1-61608-852-1

Ebook ISBN: 978-1-62914-045-2

Printed in China

Table of Contents

INTRODUCTION

While some people are born with confidence, not everyone is that fortunate. Many people have to work their entire lives to build confidence in themselves. The best way to tackle this is to work day by day to gradually achieve a solid sense of self-confidence.

A lack of confidence can come from a huge variety of sources, some external and some internal. The goal of *1,001 Pearls of Wisdom to Build Confidence* is to show those people that nothing is impossible. Whether a movie star, musician, author, artist, athlete, or politician, most people do not start at the top; they work their entire lives to reach their desired goals. Life is a constant challenge, but having faith in your own capabilities will give you the drive to know that you can achieve any goal you set. When you have confidence in yourself, you always have a friend telling you to "go for the gold." Knowing that you have the capacity for greatness will teach you that nothing is impossible. Sure, you may fail once or twice (or even more than that!), but that does not mean you are a failure. Mistakes are a wonderful thing, as they teach you what *not* to do in the future. And mistakes mean that you're challenging yourself to do new things, things you never thought possible.

All we can ask of you, dear reader, is that you believe that no matter the situation, you are capable of greatness. At times it may seem hard to believe, but believing is the first step to accepting. And once you accept this fact, then life, while always a journey, will seem less like an uphill battle.

Remember that confidence comes from inside you. While others may be able to motivate you, the only way to improve is to start at the beginning—with you.

Good luck, always keep your chin up, and never stop fighting.

1,001 PEARLS OF WISDOM TO BUILD CONFIDENCE

1

THE PSYCHOLOGY
OF CONFIDENCE

A man should not strive to eliminate his complexes but to get into accord with them: they are legitimately what directs his conduct in the world.

—Sigmund Freud

The most terrifying thing is to accept oneself completely.

—C. G. Jung

There is nothing either good or bad, but thinking makes it so.

—William Shakespeare, *Hamlet*

A clever person solves a problem. A wise person avoids it.

—Albert Einstein

Chiefly the mold of a man's fortune is in his own hands.

—Francis Bacon, *Essays*

Nothing builds self-esteem and self-confidence like accomplishment.

—Thomas Carlyle

Man is not what he thinks he is, he is what he hides.

—André Malraux

The first step toward change is awareness. The second step is acceptance.

—Nathaniel Branden

What do we mean by saying that existence precedes essence? We mean that man first of all exists, encounters himself, surges up in the world—and defines himself afterward.

—Jean-Paul Sartre, *Existentialism is a Humanism*

Don't become a mere recorder of facts, but try to penetrate the mystery of their origin.

—Ivan Pavlov

Every individual acts and suffers in accordance with his peculiar teleology, which has all the inevitability of fate, so long as he does not understand it.

—Alfred Adler, *What Life Should Mean to You*

What a man thinks of himself, that it is which determines, or rather indicates, his fate.

—Henry David Thoreau, *Walden*

The fundamental cause of trouble in the world today is that the stupid are cocksure while the intelligent are full of doubt.

—Bertrand Russell, "Christian Ethics" from *Marriage and Morals*

All you need in this life is ignorance and confidence, and then success is sure.

—Mark Twain, "Letter to Mrs. Foote"

Learn to value yourself, which means: to fight for your happiness.

—Ayn Rand

It is not the mountain we conquer but ourselves.

—Sir Edmund Hillary

We know what we are but not what we may be.

—William Shakespeare, *Hamlet*

For real self-esteem is not derived from the great things you've done, the things you won, the mark you've made, but from an appreciation of yourself for what you are.

—Dr. Maxwell Maltz

The curious paradox is that when I accept myself just as I am, then I can change.

—Carl R. Rogers

We should praise the qualities we would like to see in others, declare that others possess them already, and then watch how quickly these persons will respond.

—Catherine Ponder

Closest to the truth are those who deal lightly with it because they know it is inexhaustible.

—Golo Mann

Everyone is a reactionary about subjects he understands.

—Robert Conquest

The very exercise of leadership fosters capacity for it.

—Cyril Falls

Action springs not from thought, but from a readiness for responsibility.

—Dietrich Bonhoeffer, *A Testament to Freedom*

Being entirely honest with oneself is a good exercise.

—Sigmund Freud

The Way to do is to be.

—Lao Tzu

Self-trust is the first secret of success.

—Ralph Waldo Emerson

When there is no enemy within, the enemies
outside cannot hurt you.

—African Proverb

What lies behind us and what lies before us are tiny
matters compared to what lies within us.

—Henry S. Haskins, *Meditations in Wall Street*

A person's worth in this world is estimated
according to the value they put on themselves.

—Jean De La Bruyere

I have not failed. I have just found 10,000 things that do not work.

—Thomas Edison

Low self-esteem is like driving through life with your hand-break on.

—Dr. Maxwell Maltz

If you can keep your wits about you while others are losing theirs and blaming you, the world will be yours.

—Rudyard Kipling, "If"

Creativity exists in the spaces between ideas.

—David Wescott

A man cannot be comfortable without his own approval.

—Mark Twain

Once you become self-conscious, there is no end to it; once you start to doubt, there is no room for anything else.

—Mignon McLaughlin, *The Neurotic's Notebook*

Authority slavery is one of the biggest enemies of truth. Long live insolence! It is my guardian angel in this world.

—Albert Einstein

They are the weakest, however strong, who have no faith in themselves or their own powers.

—Christian Bovee

A wonderful fact to reflect upon, that every human creature is constituted to be that profound secret and mystery to every other.

—Charles Dickens, *A Tale of Two Cities*

I know that I am intelligent, because I know that I know nothing.

—Socrates

Self-esteem isn't everything; it's just that there's nothing without it.

—Gloria Steinem

How hurtful it can be to deny one's true self and live a life of lies just to appease others.

—June Ahern

It's all in the mind.

—George Harrison

Great spirits have often overcome violent opposition from mediocre minds.

—Albert Einstein

Change starts when someone sees the next step.

—William Drayton

You cannot be lonely if you like the person you're alone with.

—Wayne Dyer

I have great faith in fools; self-confidence my friends call it.

—Edgar Allan Poe, *Marginalia*

The human mind is not a terribly logical or consistent place.

—Jim Butcher, *Turn Coat*

Whatever is rejected from the self, appears in the world as an event.

—C. G. Jung

At thirty a man should know himself like the palm of his hand, know the exact number of his defects and qualities, know how far he can go, foretell his failures—be what he is. And, above all, accept these things.

—Albert Camus

Other people's opinion of you does not have to become your reality.

—Les Brown

Meanings are not determined by situations, but we determine ourselves by the meanings we give to situations.

—Alfred Adler, *What Life Should Mean to You*

Productive achievement is a consequence and an expression of health, self-esteem, not its cause.

—Nathaniel Branden

Leadership is doing what is right when no one is watching.

—George Van Valkenburg

We forget very easily what gives us pain.

—Graham Greene, *The Ministry of Fear*

I was always looking outside myself for strength and confidence, but it comes from within. It is there all the time.

—Anna Freud

The greatest discovery of my generation is that human beings can alter their lives by altering their attitudes of mind.

—William James

A person can't change all at once.

—Stephen King, *The Stand*

A man wrapped up in himself makes a very small parcel.

—John Ruskin

Even a happy life cannot be without a measure of darkness, and the word happy would lose its meaning if it were not balanced by sadness.

—C. G. Jung

It's not who you are that holds you back, it's what you think you are not.

—Denis Waitley

There is nothing so whole as a broken heart.

—Menachem Mendel

Happiness is when what you think, what you say, and what you do are in harmony.

—Mahatma Gandhi

Until you make the unconscious conscious, it will direct your life and you will call it fate.

—C. G. Jung

Sex appeal is fifty percent what you've got and fifty percent what people think you've got.

—Sophia Loren

It's hard to fight an enemy who has outposts in your head.

—Sally Kempton, *Esquire*

Self-esteem is the reputation we acquire with ourselves.

—Nathaniel Branden

Only the liberation of the natural capacity for love in human beings can master their sadistic destructiveness.

—Wilhelm Reich

Argue for your limitations and, sure enough, they're yours.

—Richard Bach, *Illusions*

People often say that this or that person has not yet found himself. But the self is not something one finds; it is something one creates.

—Thomas Stephen Szasz

To be authentic, you have to be everything that you are, omitting nothing. Within everyone there is light/ shadow, good/evil, love/hate.

—Deepak Chopra

It isn't normal to know what we want. It is a rare and difficult psychological achievement.

—Abraham Harold Maslow

If you doubt yourself, then indeed you stand on shaky ground.

—Henrik Ibsen

Your chances of success in any undertaking can always be measured by your belief in yourself.

—Robert Collier

A man kept his character even when he was insane.

—Graham Greene, *The Ministry of Fear*

The point is to be free, not to be crazy.

—Tsoknyi Rinpoche

Having a low opinion of yourself is not 'modesty.'
It's self-destruction. Holding your uniqueness
in high regard is not 'egotism.' It's a necessary
precondition to happiness and success.

—Bobbe Sommer

Wisdom tends to grow in proportion to one's
awareness of one's ignorance.

—Anthony de Mello, *One Minute Wisdom*

The only limits are, as always, those of vision.

—James Broughton

You gain strength, courage, and confidence by every experience in which you really stop to look fear in the face.

—Eleanor Roosevelt

I'm not okay, you're not okay, and that's okay.

—Elizabeth Kubler-Ross

Self-esteem is as necessary to the spirit as food is to the body.

—Dr. Maxwell Maltz

Optimism is an intellectual choice.

—Diana Schneider

There is no value-judgment more important to a man—no factor more decisive in his psychological development and motivation—than the estimate he passes on himself.

—Nathaniel Branden, *The Psychology of Self-Esteem*

Confidence is directness and courage in meeting the facts of life.

—John Dewey

There comes a time when you look into the mirror and you realize that what you see is all that you will ever be. And then you accept it. Or you kill yourself. Or you stop looking in mirrors.

—Tennessee Williams

By not caring too much about what people think, I'm able to think for myself and propagate ideas which are very often unpopular. And I succeed.

—Albert Ellis

When the grass looks greener on the other side of the fence, it may be that they take better care of it there.

—Cecil Selig

Hope is both the earliest and the most indispensable virtue inherent in the state of being alive. If life is to be sustained hope must remain, even where confidence is wounded, trust impaired.

—Erik Erikson

It took me a long time not to judge myself through someone else's eyes.

—Sally Field

A person can grow only as much as his horizon allows.

—John Powell

Beware of no man more than of yourself; we carry our worst enemies within us.

—G. K. Chesterton

Your visions will become clear only when you can look into your own heart. Who looks outside, dreams; who looks inside, awakes.

—C. G. Jung

Therefore do not deceive yourself! Of all deceivers fear most yourself!

—Søren Kierkegaard

The thing always happens that you really believe in; and the belief in a thing makes it happen.

—Frank Lloyd Wright

Yours is the energy that makes your world. There are no limitations to the self except those you believe in.

—Jane Roberts

2

A SPIRITUAL
APPROACH

Happiness depends upon ourselves.

—Aristotle

True wisdom comes to each of us when we realize
how little we understand about life, ourselves, and
the world around us.

—Socrates

To conquer fear is the beginning of wisdom.

—Bertrand Russell

A Spiritual Approach

Happiness is that state of consciousness which proceeds from the achievement of one's values.

—Ayn Rand

I went through a lot of phases and studied many religions. I am not into religion; I am spiritual.

—Ja Rule

I live in that solitude which is painful in youth, but delicious in the years of maturity.

—Albert Einstein

Happiness is not something ready-made. It comes from your own actions.

—Dalai Lama

Live as if you were to die tomorrow. Learn as if you were to live forever.

—Mahatma Gandhi

You yourself, as much as anybody in the entire universe, deserve your love and affection.

—Siddhārtha Gautama

The only power that exists is inside ourselves.

—Anne Rice, *Interview with the Vampire*

Every day we slaughter our finest impulses. That is why we get a heart-ache when we read those lines written by the hand of a master and recognize them as our own, as the tender shoots which we stifled because we lacked the faith to believe in our own powers, our own criterion of truth and beauty. Every man, when he gets quiet, when he becomes desperately honest with himself, is capable of uttering profound truths. We all derive from the same source. There is no mystery about the origin of things. We are all part of creation, all kings, all poets, all musicians; we have only to open up, to discover what is already there.

—Henry Miller, *Sexus*

A Spiritual Approach

Remember that wherever your heart is, there you will find your treasure.

—Paulo Coelho, *The Alchemist*

The greatest thing in the world is to know how to belong to oneself.

—Michel de Montaigne, *The Complete Essays*

The man who does not value himself cannot value anything or anyone.

—Ayn Rand, *The Virtue of Selfishness*

No one really knows why they are alive until they know what they'd die for.

—Martin Luther King Jr.

It requires more courage to suffer than to die.

—Napoleon Bonaparte

You have to liberate yourself first from the prejudices of the world in which you live.

—Donald Kagan

A Spiritual Approach

A well-written life is almost as rare as a well-spent one.

—Thomas Carlyle

Beauty is no quality in things themselves. It exists merely in the mind which contemplates them.

—David Hume, *Of the Standard of Taste and Other Essays*

Contention is inseparable from creating knowledge. It is not contention we should try to avoid, but discourses that attempt to suppress contention.

—Joyce Appleby, *A Restless Past*

Aim at heaven and you will get earth thrown in. Aim at earth and you get neither.

—C. S. Lewis, *The Joyful Christian*

Just as a candle cannot burn without fire, men cannot live without a spiritual life.

—Siddhārtha Gautama

You cannot believe in God until you believe in yourself.

—Swami Vivekananda

Morality is of the highest importance—but for us, not for God.

—Albert Einstein

A thorough knowledge of the Bible is worth more than a college education.

—Theodore Roosevelt

Preach the Gospel at all times and when necessary use words.

—Francis of Assisi

Prayer does not change God, but it changes him who prays.

—Søren Kierkegaard

I have been all things unholy. If God can work through me, he can work through anyone.

—Francis of Assisi

We are punished by our sins, not for them.

—Elbert Hubbard

Science can purify religion from error and superstition. Religion can purify science from idolatry and false absolutes.

—Pope John Paul II

Fashion is almost like a religion, for me at least.

—ASAP Rocky

Wonder is the beginning of wisdom.

—Socrates

I never knew how to worship until I knew how to love.

—Henry Ward Beecher

The glory of Christianity is to conquer by forgiveness.

—William Blake

The Bible shows the way to go to heaven, not the way the heavens go.

—Galileo Galilei

A Spiritual Approach

Wonder is the basis of worship.

—Thomas Carlyle, *Sartor Resartus*

I know the Bible is inspired because it inspires me.

—Dwight L. Moody

Prayer is the spirit speaking truth to Truth.

—Philip James Bailey

51

Prayer is aligning ourselves with the purposes of God.

—E. Stanley Jones

My life was changed in one breath from God.

—Donna Summer

Science without religion is lame; religion without science is blind.

—Albert Einstein

When I do good, I feel good. When I do bad, I feel bad. That's my religion.

—Abraham Lincoln

If you have a particular faith or religion, that is good. But you can survive without it.

—Dalai Lama

My religion is based on truth and non-violence. Truth is my God. Non-violence is the means of realizing Him.

—Mahatma Gandhi

Your daily life is your temple and your religion. When you enter into it take with you your all.

—Khalil Gibran

I have an everyday religion that works for me. Love yourself first, and everything else falls into line.

—Lucille Ball

Love is my religion—I could die for it.

—John Keats

My country is the world, and my religion is to do good.

—Thomas Paine

Joy in the universe, and keen curiosity about it all—that has been my religion.

—John Burroughs

Passion is universal humanity. Without it religion, history, romance, and art would be useless.

—Honore de Balzac

Happiness is a mystery, like religion, and should never be rationalized.

—G. K. Chesterton

Where knowledge ends, religion begins.

—Benjamin Disraeli

Every man, either to his terror or consolation, has some sense of religion.

—Heinrich Heine

A Spiritual Approach

As a teenager, I increasingly had questions about religion to which I found no good answers.

—Julian Baggini

Religion is life inspired by Heavenly Love; and life is something fresh and cheerful and vigorous.

—Lucy Larcom

Someone once told me that religion is like a knife: you can stab someone with it, or you can slice bread with it.

—Vera Farmiga

57

I'm still a person, a human being, no matter what religion I am.

—T-Pain

I do not belong to any religion. Everything is between God and myself.

—Indra Devi

So much of religion is exegesis. I would rather follow in the footprints of Christ than all of the dogma.

—Christy Turlington

You can have religion with spirituality. You can also have religion without spirituality.

—Eckhart Tolle

Difference of religion breeds more quarrels than difference of politics.

—Wendell Phillips

I'm not involved in the politics of religion, but I love what the message is.

—Jane Seymour

Educate men without religion and you make of them but clever devils.

—Arthur Wellesley

Our religion does not discriminate according to color, sex, or anything else. What counts is piety and faith.

—King Hussein I

The enemies of the Christian religion and the Law of God confuse law with faith.

—Randall Terry

Religion and modernity are not necessarily mutually exclusive.

—Queen Rania of Jordan

I think it's imperative to have faith or religion, because it's good to have morals, to be kind to others.

—Tinie Tempah

We live in a great country. It's time again to get religion about it.

—Eric Liu

61

There are always people who will—who will do peculiar things and think that they are doing things in the name of their religion.

—Feisal Abdul Rauf

I don't believe there's any inherent darkness at the center of religion at all. I think religion actually is a morally neutral force.

—Ian McEwan

God knows why—no pun intended—but every time I write a song, I feel a need to touch on religion.

—Martin Gore

I believe having religion in your life creates the potential for long-lasting relationships.

—Goldie Hawn

I have always said that often the religion you were born with becomes more important to you as you see the universality of truth.

—Ram Dass

Religion doesn't make people bigots. People are bigots and they use religion to justify their ideology.

—Reza Aslan

63

Religion is for people who are scared to go to hell. Spirituality is for people who have already been there.

—Bonnie Raitt

The contemporary form of true greatness lies in a civilization founded on the spirituality of work.

—Simone Weil

Humor is a part of spirituality.

—Zooey Deschanel

A Spiritual Approach

My grandfather was a voodoo priest. A lot of my life dealt with spirituality. I can close my eyes and remember where I come from.

—Wyclef Jean

Religion can be both good and bad—it is spirituality that counts.

—Pat Buckley

I tend to place my own value in spirituality rather than religiosity.

—Kitty Kelley

To me, spirituality means 'no matter what.' One stays on the path, one commits to love, one does ones work; one follows one's dream; one shares, tries not to judge, no matter what.

—Yehuda Berg

I liked the humor of it. I've always enjoyed a sense of humor in God and in religion and in spirituality.

—Amber Tamblyn

I also work with the spirituality of people.

—Della Reese

My driving force is spirituality.

—Debra Wilson

We should honor Mother Earth with gratitude; otherwise our spirituality may become hypocritical.

—Radhanath Swami

The new physics provides a modern version of ancient spirituality. In a universe made out of energy, everything is entangled; everything is one.

—Bruce Lipton

We are looking to brands for poetry and for spirituality, because we're not getting those things from our communities or from each other.

—Naomi Klein

When the solution is simple, God is answering.

—Albert Einstein

Never trust anyone completely but God. Love people, but put your full trust only in God.

—Lawrence Welk

God, as Truth, has been for me a treasure beyond price. May He be so to every one of us.

—Mahatma Gandhi

God has given us two hands, one to receive with and the other to give with.

—Billy Graham

God, from a beautiful necessity, is Love.

—Martin Farquhar Tupper

A thick skin is a gift from God.

—Konrad Adenauer

God is one, greatest of gods and men, not like mortals in body or thought.

—Xenophanes

God always gives His best to those who leave the choice with him.

—Jim Elliot

Before God we are all equally wise—and equally foolish.

—Albert Einstein

God gave us the gift of life; it is up to us to give ourselves the gift of living well.

—Voltaire

God has given you one face, and you make yourself another.

—William Shakespeare, *Hamlet*

You don't choose your family. They are God's gift to you, as you are to them.

—Desmond Tutu

God will never give you anything you can't handle, so don't stress.

—Kelly Clarkson

3

FOLLOWING YOUR DREAMS

Put your future in good hands—your own.

—Unknown

All men dream but not equally. Those who dream by night in the dusty recesses of their minds wake in the day to find that it was vanity; but the dreamers of the day are dangerous men, for they may act their dream with open eyes to make it possible.

—T. E. Lawrence, *Seven Pillars of Wisdom*

Be the change that you wish to see in the world.

—Mahatma Gandhi

The future belongs to those who believe in the beauty of their dreams.

—Eleanor Roosevelt

Nothing splendid has ever been achieved except by those who dared believe that something inside of them was superior to circumstance.

—Bruce Barton

Do not fear to be eccentric in opinion, for every opinion now accepted was once eccentric.

—Bertrand Russell

If you want a quality, act as if you already had it. If you want to be courageous, act as if you were—and as you act and persevere in acting, so you tend to become.

—Norman Vincent Peale

If you don't gamble, you'll never win.

—Aldous Huxley

You're damned if you're too thin and you're damned if you're too heavy. According to the press I've been both. It's impossible to satisfy everyone and I suggest we stop trying.

—Jennifer Aniston

Reality is wrong. Dreams are for real.

—Tupac Shakur

If you have no confidence in self, you are twice
defeated in the race of life. With confidence, you
have won even before you have started.

—Marcus Garvey

Painting is self-discovery. Every good painter paints
what he is.

—Jackson Pollock

Whatever you do may seem insignificant, but it is most important that you do it.

—Mahatma Gandhi

The most important kind of freedom is to be what you really are. You trade in your reality for a role. You give up your ability to feel, and in exchange, put on a mask.

—Jim Morrison

I do not believe in taking the right decision. I take a decision and make it right.

—Muhammad Ali Jinnah

Don't let anyone steal your dream. It's your dream, not theirs.

—Dan Zadr

Not to dream boldly may turn out to be simply irresponsible.

—George Leonard

You have brains in your head.
You have feet in your shoes.
You can steer yourself in any direction you choose.
You're on your own.
And you know what you know.
You are the guy who'll decide where to go.

—Dr. Seuss, *Oh, the Places You'll Go!*

Myths are public dreams; dreams are private myths.

—Joseph Campbell

Dreams are necessary to life.

—Anaïs Nin

Dream in a pragmatic way.

—Aldous Huxley

Following Your Dreams

We either make ourselves miserable, or we make ourselves strong. The amount of work is the same.

—Carlos Castaneda

I am only one, but I am one. I cannot do everything, but I can do something. And because I cannot do everything, I will not refuse to do the something that I can do.

—Edward Everett Hale

No one has ever achieved anything from the smallest to the greatest unless the dream was dreamed first.

—Laura Ingalls Wilder

Do all you can to make your dreams come true.

—Joel Osteen

Dreams are the touchstones of our character.

—Henry David Thoreau, *A Week on the Concord and Merrimack Rivers*

Go confidently in the direction of your dreams. Live the life you've imagined.

—Henry David Thoreau

The first step to getting the things you want out of life is this: Decide what you want.

—Ben Stein

Don't wait until everything is just right. It will never be perfect. There will always be challenges, obstacles, and less than perfect conditions. So what. Get started now. With each step you take, you will grow stronger and stronger, more and more skilled, more and more self-confident, and more and more successful.

—Mark Victor Hansen

Aerodynamically the bumblebee shouldn't be able to fly, but the bumblebee doesn't know that so it goes on flying anyway.

—Mary Kay Ash

Commitment leads to action. Action brings your dream closer.

—Marcia Wieder

I am a dreamer. Seriously, I'm living on another planet.

—Eva Green

The interpretation of dreams is a great art.

—Paracelsus

The biggest adventure you can take is to live the life of your dreams.

—Oprah Winfrey

There is nothing impossible to him who will try.

—Alexander the Great

It may be that the most interesting American struggle is the struggle to set oneself free from the limits one is born to, and then to learn something of the value of those limits.

—Greil Marcus

Only those who risk going too far can possibly find out how far one can go.

—T. S. Eliot

The world has the habit of making room for the man whose words and actions show that he knows where he is going.

—Napoleon Hill

Inaction breeds doubt and fear. Action breeds confidence and courage. If you want to conquer fear, do not sit home and think about it. Go out and get busy.

—Dale Carnegie

The chief danger in life is that you may take too many precautions.

—Alfred Adler

As my father used to tell me, the only true sign of success in life is being able to do for a living that which makes you happy.

—Weird Al Yankovic

How can a president not be an actor?

—Ronald Reagan

Once you've gotten the job, there's nothing to it. If you're an actor, you're an actor. Doing it is not the hard part. The hard part is getting to do it.

—Morgan Freeman

Hold fast to dreams, for if dreams die, life is a broken winged bird that cannot fly.

—Langston Hughes, "Dreams"

The history of the world is full of men who rose
to leadership, by sheer force of self-confidence,
bravery, and tenacity.

—Mahatma Gandhi

I have a theory that movies operate on the level of
dreams, where you dream yourself.

—Meryl Streep

If you really do want to be an actor who can
satisfy himself and his audience, you need to be
vulnerable.

—Jack Lemmon

The best way to make your dreams come true is to wake up.

—Paul Valery

An actor has to burn inside with an outer ease.

—Michael Chekhov

It is only through work and strife that either nation or individual moves on to greatness. The great man is always the man of mighty effort, and usually the man whom grinding need has trained to mighty effort.

—Theodore Roosevelt

Don't live down to expectations. Go out there and do something remarkable.

—Wendy Wasserstein

Man cannot discover new oceans unless he has the courage to lose sight of the shore.

—Andre Gide

Acting is all about honesty. If you can fake that, you've got it made.

—George Burns

A skillful man reads his dreams for self-knowledge, yet not the details but the quality.

—Ralph Waldo Emerson

Wanting to be someone else is a waste of the person you are.

—Marilyn Monroe

The only thing that stands between a man and what he wants from life is often merely the will to try it and the faith to believe that it is possible.

—Richard M. Devos

Following Your Dreams

Whatever you do, or dream you can, begin it.
Boldness has genius and power and magic in it.

—Johann Wolfgang von Goethe

Keep your dreams alive. Understand to achieve
anything requires faith and belief in yourself,
vision, hard work, determination, and dedication.
Remember all things are possible for those who
believe.

—Gail Devers

If you're walking down the right path and you're
willing to keep walking, eventually you'll make
progress.

—Barack Obama

Shoot for the moon. Even if you miss, you'll land among the stars.

—Les Brown

Do you want to know who you are? Don't ask. Act! Action will delineate and define you.

—Thomas Jefferson

Speak up, speak often and don't worry about those that at this point cannot understand as they can never un-hear what we tell them.

—Ron Paul

There is no passion to be found in settling for a life
that is less than the one you are capable of living.

—Nelson Mandela

Make the most of yourself, for that is all there is of
you.

—Ralph Waldo Emerson

Do what you feel in your heart to be right—for you'll
be criticized anyway. You'll be damned if you do, and
damned if you don't.

—Eleanor Roosevelt

The important thing is not being afraid to take a chance. Remember, the greatest failure is to not try. Once you find something you love to do, be the best at doing it.

—Debbi Fields

It is better to be hated for what you are, than to be loved for something you are not.

—Andre Gide, *Autumn Leaves*

Everything you want is out there waiting for you to ask. Everything you want also wants you. But you have to take action to get it.

—Jack Canfield

A man is a success if he gets up in the morning and gets to bed at night, and in between he does what he wants to do.

—Bob Dylan

Believe in something larger than yourself.

—Barbara Bush

Be who you are and say what you feel, because those who mind don't matter, and those who matter don't mind.

—Bernard M. Baruch

If you don't run your own life, somebody else will.

—John Atkinson

You must go after your wish. As soon as you start to pursue a dream, your life wakes up and everything has meaning.

—Barbara Sher, *I Could Do Anything If I Only Knew What It Was*

You can get what you want or you can just get old.

—Billy Joel, "Only the Good Die Young," *The Stranger*

Trust yourself. Create the kind of self that you will be happy to live with all your life. Make the most of yourself by fanning the tiny, inner sparks of possibility into flames of achievement.

—Golda Meir

You don't concentrate on risks. You concentrate on results. No risk is too great to prevent the necessary job from getting done.

—Chuck Yeager

In the confrontation between the stream and the rock, the stream always wins—not through strength, but through persistence.

—Siddhārtha Gautama

The secret to happiness is freedom. . . . And the secret to freedom is courage.

—Thucydides

Delay is the deadliest form of denial.

—C. Northcote Parkinson

It is precisely the possibility of realizing a dream that makes life interesting.

—Paulo Coelho, *The Alchemist*

Only the truth of who you are, if realized, will set you free.

—Eckhart Tolle

Let us dare to read, think, speak, and write.

—John Adams

Man is a genius when he is dreaming.

—Akira Kurosawa

Live daringly, boldly, fearlessly. Taste the relish to be found in competition—in having put forth the best within you.

—Henry J. Kaiser, "How to Capture Life's Greatest Values," *Reader's Digest*

In the future, everybody is going to be a director. Somebody's got to live a real life so we have something to make a movie about.

—Cameron Crowe

Great things are not accomplished by those who yield to trends and fads and popular opinion.

—Jack Kerouac

Following Your Dreams

To be yourself in a world that is constantly trying
to make you something else is the greatest
accomplishment.

—Ralph Waldo Emerson

Follow your dreams, believe in yourself, and don't
give up.

—Rachel Corrie

Whether you think you can or think you can't—you
are right.

—Henry Ford

The worst thing one can do is not to try, to be aware of what one wants and not give in to it, to spend years in silent hurt wondering if something could have materialized—never knowing.

—Jim Rohn

There is no security in this life. There is only opportunity.

—Douglas MacArthur

Working hard is great, being lazy sometimes is great, but failed potential is the worst.

—Campbell Scott

All my children have spoken for themselves since they first learned to speak, and not always with my advance approval, and I expect that to continue in the future.

—Gerald Ford

Well, if it can be thought, it can be done; a problem can be overcome.

—E. A. Bucchianeri, *Brushstrokes of a Gadfly*

Love what you do and do what you love. Don't listen to anyone else who tells you not to do it. You do what you want, what you love. Imagination should be the center of your life.

—Ray Bradbury

Dreams come true. Without that possibility, nature would not incite us to have them.

—John Updike

4

MAKING THE BEST
OF THE WORST

The worst thing that happens to you may be the best thing for you if you don't let it get the best of you.

—Will Rogers

A failure is not always a mistake; it may simply be the best one can do under the circumstances. The real mistake is to stop trying.

—B. F. Skinner

Failure is the key to success; each mistake teaches us something.

—Morihei Ueshiba

Making the Best of the Worst

I don't want to give advice to a nineteen-year-old, because I want a nineteen-year-old to make mistakes and learn from them. Make mistakes, make mistakes, make mistakes. Just make sure they're your mistakes.

—Fiona Apple

You make the best out of it you can. Nothing is ever as good or as bad as you think it will be. It's what you make of it.

—Nichole Chase, *Suddenly Royal*

Anyone who has never made a mistake has never tried anything new.

—Albert Einstein

Mistakes are a part of being human. Precious life lessons that can only be learned the hard way. Unless it's a fatal mistake, which, at least, others can learn from.

—Al Franken

Happiness is a state of mind—we are as happy as we make up our minds to be.

—Abraham Lincoln

Expect the best. Prepare for the worst. Capitalize on what comes.

—Zig Ziglar, *Trigger Events*

That which does not kill us makes us stronger.

—Friedrich Nietzsche

Creativity is allowing yourself to make mistakes. Art is knowing which ones to keep.

—Scott Adams

I only regret that I have but one life to lose for my country.

—Nathan Hale

To give up yourself without regret is the greatest charity.

—Bodhidharma

I'm not big on regret; I don't spend a lot of time on it.

—Joss Whedon

It's not what happens to you, but how you react to it that matters.

—Epictetus

The price of inaction is far greater than the cost of making a mistake.

—Meister Eckhart

If you have fear of some pain or suffering, you should examine whether there is anything you can do about it. If you can, there is no need to worry about it; if you cannot do anything, then there is also no need to worry.

—Dalai Lama

He who joyfully marches to music in rank and file has already earned my contempt. He has been given a large brain by mistake, since for him the spinal cord would suffice.

—Albert Einstein

Opportunities to find deeper powers within ourselves come when life seems most challenging.

—Joseph Campbell

And a step backward, after making a wrong turn, is a step in the right direction.

—Kurt Vonnegut, *Player Piano*

Success seems to be connected with action. Successful people keep moving. They make mistakes, but they don't quit.

—Conrad Hilton

I don't really regret anything in my life.

—Kristin Cavallari

The only things you regret are the things you don't do.

—Michael Curtiz

A smart man makes a mistake, learns from it, and never makes that mistake again. But a wise man finds a smart man and learns from him how to avoid the mistake altogether.

—Roy H. Williams

What do you first do when you learn to swim? You make mistakes, do you not? And what happens? You make other mistakes, and when you have made all the mistakes you possibly can without drowning— and some of them many times over—what do you find? That you can swim? Well—life is just the same as learning to swim! Do not be afraid of making mistakes, for there is no other way of learning how to live!

—Alfred Adler

Expect the best, plan for the worst, and prepare to be surprised.

—Denis Waitley

No experience is a cause of success or failure. We do not suffer from the shock of our experience's so-called trauma—but we make out of them just what suits our purposes.

—Alfred Adler, *Current Psychotherapies*

Mistakes, obviously, show us what needs improving. Without mistakes, how would we know what we had to work on?

—Peter McWilliams, *Life 101*

Expose yourself to your deepest fear; after that, fear has no power, and the fear of freedom shrinks and vanishes. You are free.

—Jim Morrison

Freedom is not worth having if it does not include the freedom to make mistakes.

—Mahatma Gandhi

Bad things are not the worst things that can happen to us. Nothing is the worst thing that can happen to us!

—Richard Bach, *One*

And worse I may be yet: the worst is not / So long as we can say 'This is the worst.'

—William Shakespeare, *King Lear*

You fake something until you're good at it.

—Weird Al Yankovic

Experience is the name everyone gives to their mistakes.

—Oscar Wilde, *Cecil Graham*

Nobody made a greater mistake than he who did nothing because he could do only a little.

—Edmund Burke

I had my years of struggling. Some of my shows failed miserably, and I was upset by it and it dented my confidence. But I never stopped. I kept going for it.

—Regis Philbin

I do not regret one moment of my life.

—Lillie Langtry

Defeat is not the worst of failures. Not to have tried is the true failure.

—George Edward Woodberry

A mistake is simply another way of doing things.

—Katharine Graham

Good judgment comes from experience, and experience comes from bad judgment.

—Rita Mae Brown, *Alma Mater*

The greatest mistake you can make in life is continually fearing that you'll make one.

—Elbert Hubbard, *The Note Book of Elbert Hubbard*

I never set out to be weird. It was always other people who called me weird.

—Frank Zappa

The turning point in the process of growing up is when you discover the core of strength within you that survives all hurt.

—Max Lerner, *The Unfinished Country*

Experience enables you to recognize a mistake
when you make it again.

—Franklin P. Jones

I want to thank my parents for somehow raising me
to have confidence that is disproportionate with my
looks and abilities.

—Tina Fey

I find that the best way to do things is to constantly
move forward and to never doubt anything and
keep moving forward; if you make a mistake say
you made a mistake.

—John Frusciante

You can't make yourself feel positive, but you can choose how to act, and if you choose right, it builds your confidence.

—Jaden Smith

When you find your path, you must not be afraid. You need to have sufficient courage to make mistakes. Disappointment, defeat, and despair are the tools God uses to show us the way.

—Paulo Coelho, *Brida*

Making the Best of the Worst

There are no mistakes. The events we bring
upon ourselves, no matter how unpleasant, are
necessary in order to learn what we need to learn;
whatever steps we take, they're necessary to reach
the places we've chosen to go.

—Richard Bach, *The Bridge Across Forever*

In this business, until you're known as a monster,
you're not a star.

—Bette Davis

The only man who never makes a mistake is the
man who never does anything.

—Theodore Roosevelt

The only real mistake is the one from which we learn nothing.

—Henry Ford

You must lose everything in order to gain anything.

—Brad Pitt

By seeking and blundering we learn.

—Johann Wolfgang von Goethe

We learn from failure, not from success!

—Bram Stoker, *Dracula*

Mistakes are part of the dues one pays for a full life.

—Sophia Loren

We are all born ignorant, but one must work hard to remain stupid.

—Benjamin Franklin

A life spent making mistakes is not only more honorable, but more useful than a life spent doing nothing.

—George Bernard Shaw

There comes a time when one must take a position that is neither safe, nor politic, nor popular, but he must take it because conscience tells him it is right.

—Martin Luther King Jr.

You must never feel badly about making mistakes
. . . as long as you take the trouble to learn from
them. For you often learn more by being wrong for
the right reasons than you do by being right for the
wrong reasons.

—Norton Juster, *The Phantom Tollbooth*

There's a victory, and defeat; the first and best of
victories, the lowest and worst of defeats which
each man gains or sustains at the hands not of
another, but of himself.

—Plato

We're all damaged in our own way. Nobody's perfect. I think we are all somewhat screwy, every single one of us.

—Johnny Depp

I never made a mistake in my life; at least, never one that I couldn't explain away afterwards.

—Rudyard Kipling, *Under the Deodars*

Do what you can, with what you have, where you are.

—Theodore Roosevelt

If you are going to doubt something, doubt your limits.

—Don Ward

Have no fear of perfection—you'll never reach it.

—Salvador Dalí

Take chances, make mistakes. That's how you grow. Pain nourishes your courage. You have to fail in order to practice being brave.

—Mary Tyler Moore

It is better to light a candle than curse the darkness.

—Eleanor Roosevelt

Through humor, you can soften some of the worst blows that life delivers. And once you find laughter, no matter how painful your situation might be, you can survive it.

—Bill Cosby

We're all human and we all goof. Do things that may be wrong, but do something.

—Newt Gingrich

It is the highest form of self-respect to admit our errors and mistakes and make amends for them. To make a mistake is only an error in judgment, but to adhere to it when it is discovered shows infirmity of character.

—Dale Turner

To avoid situations in which you might make mistakes may be the biggest mistake of all.

—Peter McWilliams, *Life 101*

A well-adjusted person is one who makes the same mistake twice without getting nervous.

—Alexander Hamilton

The way to develop self-confidence is to do the thing you fear.

—William Jennings Bryan

You do what you can for as long as you can, and when you finally can't, you do the next best thing. You back up but you don't give up.

—Chuck Yeager

All men make mistakes, but a good man yields when he knows his course is wrong, and repairs the evil. The only crime is pride.

—Sophocles, *Antigone*

No one is exempt from the rule that learning occurs through recognition of error.

—Alexander Lowen, *Bioenergetics*

In any moment of decision, the best thing you can do is the right thing, the next best thing is the wrong thing, and the worst thing you can do is nothing.

—Theodore Roosevelt

Persistent people begin their success where others end in failure.

—Edward Eggleston

When one has finished building one's house, one suddenly realizes that in the process one has learned something that one really needed to know in the worst way—before one began.

—Friedrich Nietzsche

Mistakes are, after all, the foundations of truth, and if a man does not know what a thing is, it is at least an increase in knowledge if he knows what it is not.

—C. G. Jung

Even in the best of lives, mistakes are made.

—Joseph J. Ellis

Unlike some politicians, I can admit to a mistake.

—Nelson Mandela

Fools say that they learn by experience. I prefer to profit by others experience.

—Otto von Bismarck

Life shrinks or expands in proportion to one's courage.

—Anaïs Nin, *Diary*

Well, we all make mistakes, dear, so just put it behind you. We should regret our mistakes and learn from them, but never carry them forward into the future with us.

—L. M. Montgomery, *Anne of Avonlea*

The successful man will profit from his mistakes and try again in a different way.

—Dale Carnegie

While one person hesitates because he feels inferior, the other is busy making mistakes and becoming superior.

—Henry C. Link

Making the Best of the Worst

The funniest thing is that all the things every director goes through, I thought I could shortcut, but there was no getting around those issues.

—George Clooney

Even a mistake may turn out to be the one thing necessary to a worthwhile achievement.

—Henry Ford

Difficulties strengthen the mind, as labor does the body.

—Lucius Annaeus Seneca

It is unwise to be too sure of one's own wisdom. It is healthy to be reminded that the strongest might weaken and the wisest might err.

—Mahatma Gandhi

To help yourself, you must be yourself. Be the best that you can be. When you make a mistake, learn from it, pick yourself up, and move on.

—Dave Pelzer

We do not learn from experience . . . we learn from reflecting on experience.

—John Dewey

We must not say every mistake is a foolish one.

—Marcus Tullius Cicero

5

LEARNING FROM THE PAST

Reason has always existed, but not always in a reasonable form.

—Karl Marx

The reading of all good books is like a conversation with the finest minds of past centuries.

—Rene Descartes

The hardest tumble a man can make is to fall over his own bluff.

—Ambrose Bierce

The worst guilt is to accept an unearned guilt.

—Ayn Rand

There are no secrets to success. It is the result of preparation, hard work, and learning from failure.

—Colin Powell

Confidence comes not from always being right but from not fearing to be wrong.

—Peter T. McIntyre

Everything that happens to you is a reflection of what you believe about yourself. We cannot outperform our level of self-esteem. We cannot draw to ourselves more than we think we are worth.

—Iyanla Vanzant

We make the oldest stories new when we succeed, and we are trapped by the old stories when we fail.

—Greil Marcus

Confidence, like art, never comes from having all the answers; it comes from being open to all the questions.

—Earl Gray Stevens

Learning from the Past

I've done a movie and a TV series, and someday I'd like to do a successful movie and a successful TV series. That would be nice.

—Weird Al Yankovic

The first time that I performed as an actor was the first day on the set of *The Fresh Prince of Bel-Air.*

—Will Smith

Life can take so many twists and turns. You can't ever count yourself out. Even if you're really afraid at some point, you can't think that there's no room for you to grow and do something good with your life.

—Portia de Rossi

I never cut class. I loved getting A's, I liked being smart. I liked being on time. I thought being smart is cooler than anything in the world.

—Michelle Obama

We must adjust to changing times and still hold to unchanging principles.

—Jimmy Carter

To look back upon history is inevitably to distort it.

—Norman Pearson

To develop and perfect and arm conscience is the
great achievement of history.

—Lord Acton

Those who cannot remember the past are
condemned to repeat it.

—George Santayana, *The Life of Reason*

The chief practical use of history is to deliver us
from plausible historical analogies.

—James Bryce

It is very hard to remember that events now long in the past were once in the future.

—Frederic William Maitland

The causes of events are ever more interesting than the events themselves.

—Marcus Tullius Cicero

The first duty of an historian is to be on guard against his own sympathies.

—James Anthony Froude

The history of the world is but the biography of great men.

—Thomas Carlyle, *The New Dictionary of Cultural Literacy*

The main thing is to make history, not to write it.

—Otto von Bismarck

The game of history is usually played by the best and the worst over the heads of the majority in the middle.

—Eric Hoffer

History repeats itself. That's one of the things wrong with history.

—Clarence Darrow

Fable is more historical than fact, because fact tells us about one man and fable tells us about a million men.

—G. K. Chesterton

The study of history requires investigation, imagination, empathy, and respect. Reverence just doesn't enter into it.

—Jill Lepore, *The Whites of Their Eyes*

Learning from the Past

Understanding the past requires pretending that
you don't know the present.

—Paul Fussell

Man in a word has no nature; what he has . . . is
history.

—Jose Ortega y Gasset

The past is a source of knowledge, and the future
is a source of hope. Love of the past implies faith in
the future.

—Stephen Ambrose, *In Fast Company*

We can be almost certain of being wrong about the future, if we are wrong about the past.

—G. K. Chesterton

Nothing endures but change.

—Heraclitus, *Lives of the Philosophers*

History books that contain no lies are extremely dull.

—Anatole France, *La Bûche* (*The Log*)

History is always written wrong, and so always needs to be rewritten.

—George Santayana

Historians are prophets with their face turned backward.

—Friedrich von Schiller

Cynicism masquerades as wisdom, but it is the farthest thing from it. Because cynics don't learn anything. Because cynicism is a self-imposed blindness, a rejection of the world because we are afraid it will hurt us or disappoint us. Cynics always say no. But saying 'yes' begins things. Saying 'yes' is how things grow. Saying 'yes' leads to knowledge. 'Yes' is for young people. So for as long as you have the strength to, say 'yes.'

—Stephen Colbert

I don't believe in learning from other people's pictures. I think you should learn from your own interior vision of things and discover, as I say, innocently, as though there had never been anybody.

—Orson Welles

A story should have a beginning, a middle, and an end . . . but not necessarily in that order.

—Jean-Luc Godard

Life can only be understood backwards, but it must be lived forwards.

—Søren Kierkegaard

The past is never where you think you left it.

—Katherine Anne Porter

161

The past is always tense, the future perfect.

—Zadie Smith

It is by no means an irrational fancy that, in a future existence, we shall look upon what we think our present existence, as a dream.

—Edgar Allan Poe

The past is a ghost, the future a dream, and all we ever have is now.

—Bill Cosby

Learning from the Past

What's past is prologue.

—William Shakespeare, *The Tempest*

No man is rich enough to buy back his past.

—Oscar Wilde

I don't f*** much with the past but I f*** plenty with the future.

—Patti Smith

People don't realize that the future is just now, but later.

—Russell Brand

Memory is a mirror that scandalously lies.

—Julio Cortázar, *Around the Day in Eighty Worlds*

It's no use going back to yesterday, because I was a different person then.

—Lewis Carroll, *Alice's Adventures in Wonderland and Through the Looking Glass*

Those who can forget the past are way ahead of
the rest of us.

—Chuck Palahniuk, *Choke*

We have to know the truth about the past to
discover out future.

—Patti Callahan Henry, *Between the Tides*

It's best to be ruthless with the past.

—Stephen King, *Rose Madder*

People from the past, have a tendency to walk back
into the present, and run over the future.

—Anthony Liccione

You must understand and learn from your past
to live your best now and be able to plan for your
future.

—Jerry Bruckner

I try to learn from the past, but I plan for the future
by focusing exclusively on the present. That's where
the fun is.

—Donald Trump

Nothing is worth more than this day.

—Johann Wolfgang von Goethe

Breathe. Let go. And remind yourself that this very moment is the only one you know you have for sure.

—Oprah Winfrey

While I take inspiration from the past, like most Americans, I live for the future.

—Ronald Reagan

Life is divided into three terms—that which was, which is, and which will be. Let us learn from the past to profit by the present, and from the present to live better in the future.

—William Wordsworth

The future depends on what we do in the present.

—Mahatma Gandhi

The present is the blocks with which we build.

—Henry Wadsworth Longfellow

Learning from the Past

Realize deeply that the present moment is all you
ever have. Make the Now the primary focus of your
life.

—Eckhart Tolle, *The Power of Now*

Losers live in the past. Winners learn from the past
and enjoy working in the present toward the future.

—Denis Waitley

No matter how much suffering you went through,
you never wanted to let go of those memories.

—Haruki Murakami

Life is very interesting. In the end, some of your greatest pains become your greatest strengths.

—Drew Barrymore

Letting go means to come to the realization that some people are a part of your history, but not a part of your destiny.

—Steve Maraboli

Change is the law of life. And those who look only to the past or present are certain to miss the future.

—John F. Kennedy

The only difference between the saint and the sinner is that every saint has a past, and every sinner has a future.

—Oscar Wilde

Thank God I found the GOOD in good-bye.

—Beyoncé Knowles, "Best Thing I Never Had," *4*

Pain will leave you, when you let go.

—Jeremy Aldana

You don't live in the past; you take a sledgehammer to it to see what stands so that you can build on it.

—Samuel L. Drew

We're all guilty of dedicating time to people who didn't value it.

—Turcois Ominek

My acupuncturist once told me that it doesn't have to hurt to work. She might have meant the needles, but I think she really meant love.

—Erica Goros, *The Daisy Chain*

If they don't walk away, we have to walk away, and sometimes we do it crying.

—Donna Lynn Hope

We would do ourselves a tremendous favor by letting go of the people who poison our spirit.

—Steve Maraboli, *Unapologetically You*

Peace of mind arrives the moment you come to peace with the contents of your mind.

—Rasheed Ogunlaru

173

Think differently, BE better!

—Darren L. Johnson

Cry. Forgive. Learn. Move on. Let your tears water the seeds of your future happiness.

—Steve Maraboli

Some people believe holding on and hanging in there are signs of great strength. However, there are times when it takes much more strength to know when to let go and then do it.

—Ann Landers

Learning from the Past

I've been burdened with blame trapped in the past
for too long. I'm moving on.

—Rascal Flatts, "I'm Movin' On," *Rascal Flatts*

I realize there's something incredibly honest about
trees in winter, how they're experts at letting things
go.

—Jeffrey McDaniel

The greatest step toward a life of simplicity is to
learn to let go.

—Steve Maraboli, *Life, the Truth, and Being Free*

Look back, and smile on perils past.

—Sir Walter Scott, *The Complete Poetical Works of
Sir Walter Scott*

A people without the knowledge of their past
history, origin, and culture is like a tree without
roots.

—Marcus Garvey

The first recipe for happiness is: avoid too lengthy
meditation on the past.

—Andre Maurois

If we open a quarrel between past and present, we shall find that we have lost the future.

—Winston Churchill

I like the dreams of the future better than the history of the past.

—Thomas Jefferson

In this bright future you can't forget your past.

—Bob Marley, "No Woman, No Cry," *Natty Dread*

The future influences the present just as much as the past.

—Friedrich Nietzsche

There's no present. There's only the immediate future and the recent past.

—George Carlin

Take time to gather up the past so that you will be able to draw from your experience and invest them in the future.

—Jim Rohn

You can never plan the future by the past.

—Edmund Burke

I know of no way of judging the future but by the past.

—Patrick Henry

If past history was all there was to the game, the richest people would be librarians.

—Warren Buffett

Whenever I think of the past, it brings back so many memories.

—Steven Wright

Most men pursue pleasure with such breathless haste that they hurry past it.

—Søren Kierkegaard

It takes a long time to bring the past up to the present.

—Franklin D. Roosevelt

Well, the future for me is already a thing of the past.

> —Bob Dylan, "Bye & Bye," *Love and Theft*

Forget the past.

> —Nelson Mandela

I haven't been faithful to my own advice in the past. I will in the future.

> —Billy Graham

What is history? An echo of the past in the future; a reflex from the future on the past.

—Victor Hugo

The past is a great place and I don't want to erase it or to regret it, but I don't want to be its prisoner either.

—Mick Jagger

6

IMPROVING RELATIONSHIPS

The heaviest penalty for declining to rule is to be ruled by someone inferior to yourself.

—Plato, *The Republic*

Everything in the world is about sex except sex. Sex is about power.

—Oscar Wilde

Love is individual to each person and I don't think you can define it before experiencing it because it isn't going to be the same for everybody.

—Zooey Deschanel

Sex is always about emotions. Good sex is about free emotions; bad sex is about blocked emotions.

—Deepak Chopra

Love is a better teacher than duty.

—Albert Einstein

I often find it's just the confidence that makes you sexy, not what your body looks like. It's how you feel about yourself that makes you sexy.

—Queen Latifah

If your brother wrongs you, remember not so much his wrong-doing, but more than ever that he is your brother.

—Epitectus

There is nothing on this earth more to be prized than true friendship.

—Thomas Aquinas

I get angry at myself for staying in relationships way too long.

—Alanis Morissette

Freedom is what you do with what's been done to you.

—Jean-Paul Sartre

I do not care so much what I am to others as I care what I am to myself.

—Michel de Montaigne, *The Complete Essays*

There is nothing enlightened about shrinking so that other people won't feel insecure around you. We are all meant to shine, as children do.

—Marianne Williamson

Let others determine your worth and you're already lost, because no one wants people worth more than themselves.

—Peter V. Brett, *The Warded Man*

No name-calling truly bites deep unless, in some dark part of us, we believe it. If we are confident enough then it is just noise.

—Laurell K. Hamilton, *A Stroke of Midnight*

A competent and self-confident person is incapable of jealousy in anything. Jealousy is invariably a symptom of neurotic insecurity.

—Robert Heinlein, *Time Enough for Love*

When you're different, sometimes you don't see the millions of people who accept you for what you are. All you notice is the person who doesn't.

—Jodi Picoult, *Change of Heart*

As long as you look for someone else to validate who you are by seeking their approval, you are setting yourself up for disaster. You have to be whole and complete in yourself. No one can give you that. You have to know who you are—what others say is irrelevant.

—Nic Sheff, *Tweak*

You don't have to be naked to be sexy.

—Nicole Kidman

I have to fight to get what I want. I'm obsessed with showing everyone I'm really not who they think I am.

—Keira Knightly

Anyone who has the power to make you believe absurdities has the power to make you commit injustices.

—Voltaire

Love comes more naturally to the human heart than its opposite.

—Nelson Mandela, *Long Walk to Freedom*

The meeting of two personalities is like the contact of two chemical substances: if there is any reaction, both are transformed.

—C. G. Jung, *Modern Man in Search of a Soul*

For the two of us, home isn't a place. It is a person. And we are finally home.

—Stephanie Perkins, *Anna and the French Kiss*

If conversation was the lyrics, laughter was the music, making time spent together a melody that could be replayed over and over without getting stale.

—Nicholas Sparks, *The Notebook*

Every man I meet wants to protect me. I can't figure out what from.

—Mae West

Women cannot complain about men anymore until they start getting better taste in them.

—Bill Maher

One of my main regrets in life is giving considerable thought to inconsiderate people.

—Jarod Kintz, *This Book is Not for Sale*

I know enough to know that no woman should ever marry a man who hated his mother.

—Martha Gellhorn, *Selected Letters*

Our wounds are often the openings into the best and most beautiful part of us.

—David Richo

He loved her for almost everything she was and she decided that was enough to let him stay for a very long time.

—Brian Andreas, *Story People*

When we face pain in relationships our first response is often to sever bonds rather than to maintain commitment.

—bell hooks, *All About Love*

And no one will listen to us until we listen to ourselves.

—Marianne Williamson

The most painful thing is losing yourself in the process of loving someone too much, and forgetting that you are special too.

—Ernest Hemingway, *Men Without Women*

A fit, healthy body—that is the best fashion statement.

—Jess C. Scott

Assumptions are the termites of relationships.

—Henry Winkler

There is greatness in doing something you hate for the sake of someone you love.

—Shmuley Boteach

If you need something from somebody, always give that person a way to hand it to you.

—Sue Monk Kidd, *The Secret Life of Bees*

You can't lose something you never had.

—Kate Hudson

A friend is someone whose face you can see in the dark.

—Frances O'Roark Dowell, *The Secret Language of Girls*

Being single doesn't mean you're weak; it means that you're strong enough to wait for the right person.

—Niall Horan

Men are jealous of every woman, even when they don't have the slightest interest in her themselves.

—Jan Neruda

Trust is the glue of life. It's the most essential ingredient in effective communication. It's the foundational principle that holds all relationships.

—Stephen R. Covey

Real magic in relationships means an absence of judgment of others.

—Wayne Dyer

People who have good relationships at home are more effective in the marketplace.

—Zig Ziglar

Treasure your relationships, not your possessions.

—Anthony J. D'Angelo

Be honest, brutally honest. That is what's going to maintain relationships.

—Lauryn Hill

Cherish your human connections: your relationships with friends and family.

—Joseph Brodsky

When I got my first television set, I stopped caring so much about having close relationships.

—Andy Warhol

My belief is that communication is the best way to create strong relationships.

—Jada Pinkett Smith

Relationships are the hallmark of the mature person.

—Brian Tracy

Before machines the only form of entertainment people really had was relationships.

—Douglas Coupland

Relationships are like traffic lights. And I just have this theory that I can only exist in a relationship if it's a green light.

—Taylor Swift

Personal relationships are the fertile soil from which all advancement, all success, all achievement in real life grows.

—Ben Stein

What I find so interesting about people is the choices they make, and how that affects their behavior, their sense of self, and their relationships.

—Laura Linney

203

I'm just learning who I am and how relationships work and how to make them function. No different from anyone else.

—Drew Barrymore

I collect human relationships very much the way others collect fine art.

—Jerzy Kosinski

Ultimately, running a band is about the relationships you have with people.

—Billy Corgan

Improving Relationships

I would never cheapen my relationships by talking about them.

—Kristen Stewart

We waste time looking for the perfect lover, instead of creating the perfect love.

—Tom Robbins

Fighting for peace is like screwing for virginity.

—George Carlin

We are all born sexual creatures, thank God, but it's a pity so many people despise and crush this natural gift.

—Marilyn Monroe

Relationships based on obligation lack dignity.

—Wayne Dyer

Sex without love is as hollow and ridiculous as love without sex.

—Hunter S. Thompson

I have crushes on women all the time. I don't have intimate relationships with them, but I find women beautiful.

—Adam Lambert

No woman gets an orgasm from shining the kitchen floor.

—Betty Friedan, *The Feminine Mystique*

Sex is kicking death in the ass while singing.

—Charles Bukowski

Sex is an emotion in motion.

—Mae West

I believe that sex is one of the most beautiful, natural, wholesome things that money can buy.

—Steve Martin

Clinton lied. A man might forget where he parks or where he lives, but he never forgets oral sex, no matter how bad it is.

—Barbara Bush

I couldn't possibly have sex with someone with such a slender grasp on grammar!

—Russell Brand

Sick and perverted always appeals to me.

—Madonna

Physics is like sex: sure, it may give some practical results, but that's not why we do it.

—Richard P. Feynman

What holds the world together, as I have learned from bitter experience, is sexual intercourse.

—Henry Miller, *Tropic of Capricorn*

Sex pretty much cures everything.

—Chuck Palahniuk, *Choke*

If Jack's in love, he's no judge of Jill's beauty.

—Benjamin Franklin

If a man doesn't know how to dance he doesn't
know how to make love, there I said it!

—Craig Ferguson

Anybody who believes that the way to a man's
heart is through his stomach flunked geography.

—Robert Byrne

Never sleep with someone whose troubles are
worse than your own.

—Nelson Algren

Keep love in your heart. A life without it is like a sunless garden when the flowers are dead.

—Oscar Wilde

I definitely believe that if you stop working at relationships, they go away.

—Ashton Kutcher

At the touch of love everyone becomes a poet.

—Plato, *Symposium*

Sometimes the heart sees what is invisible to the eye.

—H. Jackson Brown Jr.

Immature love says: 'I love you because I need you.' Mature love says 'I need you because I love you.'

—Erich Fromm, *The Art of Loving*

Where there is love there is life.

—Mahatma Gandhi

Let us always meet each other with smile, for the smile is the beginning of love.

—Mother Teresa

If you live to be a hundred, I want to live to be a hundred minus one day so I never have to live without you.

—A. A. Milne, *Winnie-the-Pooh*

Gravitation is not responsible for people falling in love.

—Albert Einstein

A flower cannot blossom without sunshine, and man cannot live without love.

—Max Muller

Love is like war: easy to begin but very hard to stop.

—H. L. Mencken

A woman knows the face of the man she loves as a sailor knows the open sea.

—Honore de Balzac

Love is life. And if you miss love, you miss life.

—Leo Buscaglia, *Speaking of Love*

Do all things with love.

—Og Mandino

The best thing to hold onto in life is each other.

—Audrey Hepburn

The best proof of love is trust.

—Dr. Joyce Brothers

A very small degree of hope is sufficient to cause the birth of love.

—Stendhal

Only do what your heart tells you.

—Princess Diana

217

If you want to be loved, be lovable.

—Ovid, *The Art of Love*

To love another person is to see the face of God.

—Victor Hugo, *Les Misérables*

7

WORKPLACE
CONFIDENCE

A good decision is based on knowledge and not on numbers.

—Plato

One of the great things about being a director as a life choice is that it can never be mastered. Every story is its own kind of expedition, with its own set of challenges.

—Ron Howard

Ability will never catch up with the demand for it.

—Confucius

The more I want to get something done, the less I call it work.

—Richard Bach, *Illusions*

You don't need to be defined by your job.

—Weird Al Yankovic

An actor is supposed to be a sensitive instrument.

—Marilyn Monroe

The greatest leader is not necessarily the one who does the greatest things. He is the one that gets the people to do the greatest things.

—Ronald Reagan

I'm a great believer in luck, and I find the harder I work, the more I have of it.

—Thomas Jefferson

People have forgotten how to tell a story. Stories don't have a middle or an end anymore. They usually have a beginning that never stops beginning.

—Steven Spielberg

I love all sides of the work, but that doesn't mean it isn't hard.

—David McCullough

The film industry is about saying 'no' to people, and inherently you cannot take 'no' for an answer.

—James Cameron

One of the things you do as a writer and as a filmmaker is grasp for resonant symbols and imagery without necessarily fully understanding it yourself.

—Christopher Nolan

Anytime I make a movie, I really have absolutely no idea how it's going to go over. I've had the whole range of different kinds of reactions.

—Wes Anderson

Knowledge is power.

—Francis Bacon

Cinema is a matter of what's in the frame and what's out.

—Martin Scorsese

For any director with a little lucidity, masterpieces are films that come to you by accident.

—Sidney Lumet

I'm a storyteller—that's the chief function of a director. And they're moving pictures, let's make 'em move!

—Howard Hawks

A career is a series of ups and downs, of comebacks.

—Steve Guttenberg

I could never be a career politician, because I believe in telling the truth.

—Jesse Ventura

I steal from every movie ever made.

—Quentin Tarantino

I'm not the smartest fellow in the world, but I can sure pick smart colleagues.

—Franklin D. Roosevelt

Anybody can direct a picture once they know the fundamentals. Directing is not a mystery; it's not an art. The main thing about directing is: photograph the people's eyes.

—John Ford

I've learned that making a 'living' is not the same thing as making a life.

—Maya Angelou

What would you do if you weren't afraid?

—Sheryl Sandberg

Begin somewhere. You cannot build a reputation on what you intend to do.

—Liz Smith

I think the most liberating thing I did early on was to free myself from any concern with my looks as they pertained to my work.

—Meryl Streep

When they asked me what I wanted to be I said I didn't know.

—Sylvia Plath

Choose a job you love, and you will never have to work a day in your life.

—Confucius

The career of motherhood and homemaking is beyond value and needs no justification. Its importance is incalculable.

—Katherine Short

The home is the ultimate career. All other careers exist for one purpose, and that is to support the ultimate career.

—C. S. Lewis

Pitting your dream against someone else's is a fantastic way to get discouraged and depressed.

—Jon Acuff

I'm either going to be a writer or a bum.

—Carl Sandburg

I'll always be there because I'm a skilled professional actor. Whether or not I've any talent is beside the point.

—Michael Caine

When one door closes another opens but all too often there is a long hallway in between.

—Rick Jarow

Know the difference between your hobbies and your passions.

—B. S. Wood

Some people make enough, some people don't, and it has nothing to do with their paycheck.

—Janene Murphy

233

If you find yourself in a hole, stop digging.

—Sharon Cooke Vargas

School fools a lot of people. Professionally, one thing is not the most that one person can be.

—Mokokoma Mokhonoana

Being instinctively lazy, I see no point in working longer hours just to get out of debt!

—L. G. Durand

Don't confuse having a career with having a life.

—Hillary Rodham Clinton

Work to become, not to acquire.

—Elbert Hubbard

You can't build a reputation on what you're going to do.

—Confucius

If it can be written, or thought, it can be filmed.

—Stanley Kubrick

A mind troubled by doubt cannot focus on the course to victory.

—Arthur Golden

If you can DREAM it, you can DO it.

—Walt Disney

Failure doesn't mean you are a failure; it just means you haven't succeeded yet.

—Robert H. Schuller

Desire! That's the one secret of every man's career. Not education. Not being born with hidden talents. Desire.

—Johnny Carson

Dreams are extremely important. You can't do it unless you imagine it.

—George Lucas

237

I want to look back on my career and be proud of the work, and be proud that I tried everything.

—Jon Stewart

Our greatest weakness lies in giving up. The most certain way to succeed is always to try just one more time.

—Thomas Edison

Find out what you like doing best and get someone to pay you for doing it.

—Katherine Whitehorn

Success is how high you bounce when you hit bottom.

—General George S. Patton

The reward of a thing well done is to have done it.

—Ralph Waldo Emerson, *Nominalist and Realist*

Criticism of others is futile and if you indulge in it often you should be warned that it can be fatal to your career.

—Benjamin F. Fairless

Don't set compensation as a goal. Find work you like, and the compensation will follow.

—Dale Carnegie

Ideas without action are worthless.

—Khalil Gibran

Consult not your fears but your hopes and your dreams. Think not about your frustrations, but about your unfulfilled potential. Concern yourself not with what you tried and failed in, but with what it is still possible for you to do.

—Bobby Unser

If you wish to achieve worthwhile things in your personal and career life, you must become a worthwhile person in your own self-development.

—Pope John XXIII

I think everyone should experience defeat at least once during their career. You learn a lot from it.

—Brian Tracy

Attempt the impossible in order to improve your work.

—Mark Twain

When defeat comes, accept it as a signal that your plans are not sound, rebuild those plans, and set sail once more toward your coveted goal.

—Hamilton Holt

Analyzing what you haven't got as well as what you have is a necessary ingredient of a career.

—Oscar Wilde

The way you give your name to others is a measure of how much you like and respect yourself.

—Calvin Coolidge

Workplace Confidence

The world is full of willing people, some willing to work, the rest willing to let them.

—William Patten

Hard work means prosperity; only a fool idles away his time.

—Earl Nightingale

Every man's work, whether it be literature or music or pictures or architecture or anything else, is always a portrait of himself.

—Vincent van Gogh

Never put off till tomorrow what you can do today.

—Thomas Jefferson

The definition of insanity is doing the same thing over and over and expecting different results.

—Benjamin Franklin

We don't make movies to make money; we make money to make more movies.

—Walt Disney

Do one thing every day that scares you.

—Eleanor Roosevelt

When one door closes, another opens; but we often look so long and so regretfully upon the closed door that we do not see the one which has opened for us.

—Alexander Graham Bell

Success doesn't come to you; you go to it.

—Marva Collins

Every experience in your life is being orchestrated to teach you something you need to know to move forward.

—Brian Tracy

If you don't like something, change it. If you can't change it, change your attitude.

—Maya Angelou

Opportunities don't often come along. So, when they do, you have to grab them.

—Audrey Hepburn

Don't be afraid to fail. Don't waste energy trying to cover up failure. Learn from your failures and go on to the next challenge. It's OK to fail. If you're not failing, you're not growing.

—H. Stanley Judd

Big jobs usually go to the men who prove their ability to outgrow small ones.

—Ralph Waldo Emerson

One important key to success is self-confidence. An important key to self-confidence is preparation.

—Arthur Ashe

Those who do not learn from history are doomed to repeat it.

—George Santayana, *The Life of Reason*

All labor that uplifts humanity has dignity and importance and should be undertaken with painstaking excellence.

—Martin Luther King Jr.

All our dreams can come true, if we have the courage to pursue them.

—Walt Disney

It is the working man who is the happy man. It is the idle man who is the miserable man.

—Benjamin Franklin

All things are difficult before they are easy.

—Thomas Fuller

The best preparation for good work tomorrow is to do good work today.

—Elbert Hubbard

There is no substitute for hard work.

—Thomas Edison

Laziness may appear attractive, but work gives satisfaction.

—Anne Frank, *The Diary of Anne Frank*

Let the beauty of what you love be what you do.

—Rumi

It is your work in life that is the ultimate seduction.

—Pablo Picasso

Workplace Confidence

When a man tells you that he got rich through hard work, ask him: 'Whose?'

—Don Marquis

Every noble work is at first impossible.

—Thomas Carlyle, *Past and Present*

The only way to enjoy anything in this life is to earn it first.

—Ginger Rogers

By the work one knows the workman.

—Jean de La Fontaine, *Fables*

Work isn't to make money; you work to justify life.

—Marc Chagall

The greatest teacher I know is the job itself.

—James Cash Penney

Thunder is good, thunder is impressive; but it is lightning that does the work.

—Mark Twain, *Letter to an Unidentified Person*

Nothing will work unless you do.

—Maya Angelou

8

LIVING THE LIFE

A day without laughter is a day wasted.

—Nicolas Chamfort, *Historique, Politique et Litteraire*

I have a confidence about my life that comes from standing tall on my own two feet.

—Jane Fonda

Live to the point of tears.

—Albert Camus

Living the Life

If you end up with a boring, miserable life because
you listened to your mom, your dad, your teacher,
your priest, or some guy on television telling you
how to do your shit, then you deserve it.

—Frank Zappa

Be thankful that you have a life, and forsake your
vain and presumptuous desire for a second one.

—Richard Dawkins

Of all forms of caution, caution in love is perhaps
the most fatal to true happiness.

—Bertrand Russell

257

If you love everything, you will perceive the divine mystery in things.

—Fyodor Dostoevsky, *The Brothers Karamazov*

The prime necessities for success in life are money, athleticism, tailor-made clothes, and a charming smile.

—George Orwell

People shouldn't be ashamed of what they are. And it will help them, to gain self-esteem and confidence.

—M. F. Moonzajer

There is no magic cure, no making it all go away forever. There are only small steps upward: an easier day, an unexpected laugh, a mirror that doesn't matter anymore.

—Laurie Halse Anderson, *Wintergirls*

If you're old, don't try to change yourself, change your environment.

—B. F. Skinner

Good actors I've worked with all started out making faces in a mirror, and you keep making faces all your life.

—Bette Davis

259

In Hollywood if you don't have a shrink, people think you're crazy.

—Johnny Carson

You simply have to put one foot in front of the other and keep going. Put blinders on and plow right ahead.

—George Lucas

The less you reveal, the more people can wonder.

—Emma Watson

Living the Life

You only live once, but if you do it right, once is enough.

—Mae West

In three words I can sum up everything I've learned about life: it goes on.

—Robert Frost

There's nothing more boring than unintelligent actors, because all they have to talk about is themselves and acting. There have to be other things.

—Tim Robbins

Acting is standing up naked and turning around very slowly.

—Rosalind Russell

Laugh at yourself, but don't ever aim your doubt at yourself. Be bold. When you embark for strange places, don't leave any of yourself safely on shore. Have the nerve to go into unexplored territory.

—Alan Alda

I used to be self-conscious about my height, but then I thought, f*** that, I'm Harry Potter.

—Daniel Radcliffe

Happiness and moral duty are inseparably connected.

—George Washington

I don't stop when I'm tired. I only stop when I'm done.

—Marilyn Monroe

What is success? I think it is a mixture of having a flair for the thing that you are doing, knowing that it is not enough, that you have got to have hard work and a certain sense of purpose.

—Margaret Thatcher

You wouldn't worry so much about what others think of you if you realized how seldom they do.

—Eleanor Roosevelt

You have to have confidence in your ability, and then be tough enough to follow through.

—Rosalynn Carter

The stars that have most glory have no rest.

—Samuel Daniel

Those who know how to win are much more numerous than those who know how to make proper use of their victories.

—Polybius

Never dull your shine for somebody else.

—Tyra Banks

You're always with yourself, so you might as well enjoy the company.

—Diane von Fürstenberg

Give them pleasure. The same pleasure they have when they wake up from a nightmare.

—Alfred Hitchcock

Hope for the best. Expect the worst. Life is a play. We're unrehearsed.

—Mel Brooks

Style is knowing who you are, what you want to say, and not giving a damn.

—Orson Welles

Living the Life

Do the right thing.

—Spike Lee, *Do the Right Thing*

In England, I'm a horror movie director. In Germany, I'm a filmmaker. In the United States, I'm a bum.

—John Carpenter

Most folks are as happy as they make up their minds to be.

—Abraham Lincoln

If a million people see my movie, I hope they see a million different movies.

—Quentin Tarantino

A lot of times you get credit for stuff in your movie you didn't intend to be in there.

—Spike Lee

I love making people laugh. It's an addiction and it's probably dysfunctional, but I am addicted to it and there's no greater pleasure for me than sitting in a theater and feeling a lot of people losing control of themselves.

—Jay Roach

Living the Life

I think it's a very strange question that I have to defend myself. I don't feel that. You are all my guests, it's not the other way around, that's how I feel.

—Lars von Trier

My old drama coach used to say, 'Don't just do something, stand there.' Gary Cooper wasn't afraid to do nothing.

—Clint Eastwood

I have no special talents. I am only passionately curious.

—Albert Einstein

The greatness of a man is not in how much wealth he acquires, but in his integrity and his ability to affect those around him positively.

—Bob Marley

The only person who can pull me down is myself, and I'm not going to let myself pull me down anymore.

—C. JoyBell C.

If you can't get a miracle, become one.

—Nick Vujicic, *Life Without Limits*

Living the Life

It is better to travel, than to arrive.

—Siddhārtha Gautama

I believe you make your day. You make your life. So much of it is all perception, and this is the form that I built for myself. I have to accept it and work within those compounds, and it's up to me.

—Brad Pitt

Sometimes life just walks up to you, excuses itself, and punches you in the face.

—Mike Kunda

Do not focus only on your needs; focus on your purpose.

—Deborah Brodie

Difficulties come when you don't pay attention to life's whisper. Life always whispers to you first, but if you ignore the whisper, sooner or later you'll get a scream.

—Oprah Winfrey

How beautiful a day can be, when kindness touches it!

—George Elliston

Living the Life

Today is life—the only life you are sure of. Make the most of today.

—Dale Carnegie

Casting sometimes is fate and destiny more than skill and talent, from a director's point of view.

—Steven Spielberg

Sometimes the only way to ever find yourself is to get completely lost.

—Kellie Elmore

If I go a little over the top sometimes, don't worry: that's where all the sunshine is.

—Michael Treanor

The ultimate inspiration is the deadline.

—Nolan Bushnell

If people make fun of you, you must be doing something right.

—Amy Lee

A person may be proud without being vain. Pride relates more to our opinion of ourselves, vanity to what we would have others think of us.

—Jane Austen, *Pride and Prejudice*

Without wonder and insight, acting is just a business. With it, it becomes creation.

—Bette Davis

I am happy for the first in my life, I can report that I am standing on an incline instead of an edge.

—Erica Goros

I want to live like there's no tomorrow. Love like I'm on borrowed time. It's good to be alive.

—Jason Gray

You must give up the life you planned in order to have the life that is waiting for you.

—Joseph Campbell

Always be a first-rate version of yourself instead of a second-rate version of someone else.

—Judy Garland

276

Character is doing the right thing when nobody is looking.

—J. C. Watts

Don't go around saying the world owes you a living. The world owes you nothing. It was here first.

—Mark Twain

Only those who will risk going too far can possibly find out how far one can go.

—T. S. Eliot, Preface to *Transit of Venus*

Opportunity is missed by people because it is dressed in overalls and looks like work.

—Thomas Edison

When the power of love overcomes the love of power, the world will know peace.

—Jimi Hendrix

The weak can never forgive. Forgiveness is the attribute of the strong.

—Mahatma Gandhi

Living the Life

In the middle of difficulty lies opportunity.

—Albert Einstein

Do what you haven't done is the key, I think.

—Ridley Scott

Nothing can bring you peace but yourself.

—Ralph Waldo Emerson

No one can make you feel inferior without your consent.

—Eleanor Roosevelt

If it scares you, it might be a good thing to try.

—Seth Godin

I, myself, am made entirely of flaws, stitched together with good intentions.

—Augusten Burroughs, *Magical Thinking*

Only those who dare to fail greatly can ever achieve greatly.

—Robert F. Kennedy

Living the Life

I was always very comfortable with who I was.
Confident. I've never looked at my body in a
negative way.

—Jennifer Lopez

You may have a fresh start at any moment you
choose, for this thing we call 'failure' is not the
falling down, but the staying down.

—Mary Pickford, *Why Not Try God?*

The only way to do great work is to love what you
do. If you haven't found it yet, keep looking. Don't
settle.

—Steve Jobs

Always remember, your focus determines your reality.

—George Lucas

Build your own dreams, or someone else will hire you to build theirs.

—Farrah Gray

It is never too late to be what you might have been.

—George Eliot

282

Living the Life

The best way to predict the future is to invent it.

—Alan Kay

If opportunity doesn't knock, build a door.

—Milton Berle

A journey of a thousand leagues begins with one's feet.

—Lao Tzu

Logic will get you from A to B. Imagination will take you everywhere.

—Albert Einstein

One person's craziness is another person's reality.

—Tim Burton

In matters of style, swim with the current; in matters of principle, stand like a rock.

—Thomas Jefferson

It wasn't raining when Noah built the ark.

—Howard Ruff

Living the Life

The only thing worse than being blind is having sight but no vision.

—Helen Keller

Don't go through life, grow through life.

—Eric Butterworth

I am an optimist. It does not seem too much use being anything else.

—Winston Churchill

The only way to have a friend is to be one.

—Ralph Waldo Emerson, *Essays*

I don't know the key to success, but the key to failure is trying to please everybody.

—Bill Cosby

Do not anticipate trouble, or worry about what may never happen. Keep in the sunlight.

—Benjamin Franklin

9

CONFIDENCE ON THE FIELD

I learned that if you want to make it bad enough, no matter how bad it is, you can make it.

—Gayle Sayers

The mark of a great player is in his ability to come back. The great champions have all come back from defeat.

—Sam Snead

If you can believe it, the mind can achieve it.

—Ronnie Lott

Every season has its peaks and valleys. What you have to try to do is eliminate the Grand Canyon.

—Andy Van Slyke

You're always going to survive the pain of loss. I can live with that confidence inside of me.

—Hope Solo

I think exercise tests us in so many ways, our skills, our hearts, our ability to bounce back after setbacks. This is the inner beauty of sports and competition, and it can serve us all well as adult athletes.

—Peggy Fleming

Persistence can change failure into extraordinary achievement.

—Matt Biondi

You've got to believe you can get a result from the game.

—Gary Speed

It's not whether you get knocked down; it's whether you get up.

—Vince Lombardi

The potential elite runner must realize that hard means hard, easy means easy, and they must patiently seek out what combinations work for them. They have to learn to be persistent and patient with their training and racing.

—Frank Shorter

Never let up. The more you can win by, the more doubts you put in the other players' minds the next time out.

—Sam Snead

I've missed more than 9,000 shots in my career.
I've lost almost 300 games. 26 times, I've been
trusted to take the game winning shot and missed.
I've failed over and over and over again in my life.
And that is why I succeed.

—Michael Jordan

He who is not courageous enough to take risks will
accomplish nothing in life.

—Muhammad Ali

Confidence on the Field

There may be people that have more talent than you, but there's no excuse for anyone to work harder than you do.

—Derek Jeter

If you come to a fork in the road, take it.

—Yogi Berra

Judgment traps you within the limitations of your comparisons. It inhibits freedom.

—Willie Stargell

295

The best kids are going to become the best. But the best thing about it is that you're going to learn lessons in playing those sports about winning and losing and teamwork and teammates and arguments and everything else that are going to affect you positively for the rest of your life.

—Carl Lewis

You can't put a limit on anything. The more you dream, the farther you get.

—Michael Phelps

You miss 100 percent of the shots you don't take.

—Wayne Gretzky

I'm a dreamer. I have to dream and reach for the stars, and if I miss a star then I grab a handful of clouds.

—Mike Tyson

Bodybuilding is much like any other sport. To be successful, you must dedicate yourself 100 percent to your training, diet, and mental approach.

—Arnold Schwarzenegger

Correct one fault at a time. Concentrate on the one fault you want to overcome.

—Sam Snead

A champion is someone who gets up when he can't.

—Jack Dempsey

The more I talk to athletes, the more convinced I become that the method of training is relatively unimportant. There are many ways to the top, and the training method you choose is just the one that suits you best. No, the important thing is the attitude of the athlete, the desire to get to the top.

—Herb Elliott

The five S's of sports training are: stamina, speed, strength, skill, and spirit; but the greatest of these is spirit.

—Ken Doherty

To succeed . . . you need to find something to hold on to, something to motivate you, something to inspire you.

—Tony Dorsett

To be the man, you have to beat the man.

—Ric Flair

I've had to learn to fight all my life—got to learn to keep smiling. If you smile things will work out.

—Serena Williams

Do I consider myself sexy? It all depends on the way I'm feeling. When I'm happy inside, that's when I feel most sexy.

—Anna Kournikova

When you have confidence, you can do anything.

—Sloane Stephens

The only way to prove that you're a good sport is to lose.

—Ernie Banks

Heroes get remembered, but legends never die.

—Babe Ruth

You win a few, you lose a few. Some get rained out. But you got to dress for all of them.

—Satchel Paige

Confidence is contagious. So is lack of confidence.

—Vince Lombardi

Sometimes you've got to go through hell to get to heaven.

—Dean Karnazes

I eventually became proud of my strikeouts, because each one represented another learning experience.

—Willie Stargell

No matter how good you get you can always get better, and that's the exciting part.

—Tiger Woods

An athlete cannot run with money in his pockets. He must run with hope in his heart and dreams in his head.

—Emil Zatopek

The quality of a man's life is in direct proportion to his commitment to excellence.

—Tom Landry

I think it's my personality to overcome things, learn from them, and become stronger, both personally and professionally. To be honest, I welcome those hardships.

—Hope Solo

Some people want it to happen, some wish it would happen, and others make it happen.

—Michael Jordan

I may have been fierce, but never low or underhand.

—Ty Cobb

Show me a guy who's afraid to look bad, and I'll show you a guy you can beat every time.

—Lou Brock

Winners never quit and quitters never win.

—Vince Lombardi

The difference between the impossible and the possible lies in a person's determination.

—Tommy Lasorda

I've been in a poor physical shape many times in my career and I've had some of my best results. My best performances happened because my mind was in the right place. The mind is definitely stronger than the body.

—Kelly Slater

In the end, it's extra effort that separates a winner from second place. But winning takes a lot more than that, too. It starts with complete command of the fundamentals. Then it takes desire, determination, discipline, and self-sacrifice. And finally, it takes a great deal of love, fairness, and respect for your fellow man. Put all these together, and even if you don't win, how can you lose?

—Jesse Owens

306

Confidence on the Field

I do what I want.

—Li Na

One man can be a crucial ingredient on a team, but one man cannot make a team.

—Kareem Abdul-Jabbar

You never have to wait long, or look far, to be reminded of how thin the line is between being a hero or a goat.

—Mickey Mantle

Sports teaches you character, it teaches you to play by the rules, it teaches you to know what it feels like to win and lose—it teaches you about life.

—Billie Jean King

Age is no barrier. It's a limitation you put on your mind.

—Jackie Joyner-Kersee

To be consistently effective, you must put a certain distance between yourself and what happens to you on the golf course. This is not indifference; it's detachment.

—Sam Snead

Athletic competition clearly defines the unique
power of our attitude.

—Bart Starr

You only ever grow as a human being if you're
outside your comfort zone.

—Percy Cerutty

Every strike brings me closer to the next home run.

—Babe Ruth

When you've got something to prove, there's nothing greater than a challenge.

—Terry Bradshaw

Being properly prepared is one of the biggest assets in business and in athletic competition.

—Keeth Smart

I don't know anything that builds the will to win better than competitive sports.

—Richard M. Nixon

Somewhere behind the athlete you've become and the hours of practice and the coaches who have pushed you is a little girl who fell in love with the game and never looked back . . . play for her.

—Mia Hamm

It's not the will to win that matters—everyone has that. It's the will to prepare to win that matters.

—Paul "Bear" Bryant

Continuous effort—not strength or intelligence—is the key to unlocking our potential.

—Liane Cardes

Never give up, never give in, and when the upper hand is ours, may we have the ability to handle the win with the dignity that we absorbed the loss.

—Doug Williams

I've learned that something constructive comes from every defeat.

—Tom Landry

If you can't outplay them, outwork them.

—Ben Hogan

312

Persistence can change failure into extraordinary achievement.

—Marv Levy

The road to Easy Street goes through the sewer.

—John Madden

You've got to take the initiative and play your game. In a decisive set, confidence is the difference.

—Chris Evert

What other people may find in poetry or art museums, I find in the flight of a good drive.

—Arnold Palmer

We are all born naked into this world, but each of us is fully clothed in potential.

—Emmitt Smith

Success is where preparation and opportunity meet.

—Bobby Unser

You have to do something in your life that is honorable and not cowardly if you are to live in peace with yourself.

—Larry Brown

What makes something special is not just what you have to gain, but what you feel there is to lose.

—Andre Agassi

It's very important that you focus on winning games and being consistent down the stretch. I think that's what we're focused on. All of the other stuff about who wins and who loses and how many wins do we need, if we're focusing on that, then that's not good.

—Mike Singletary

I've worked too hard and too long to let anything stand in the way of my goals. I will not let my teammates down, and I will not let myself down.

—Mia Hamm

Always make a total effort, even when the odds are against you.

—Arnold Palmer

Push yourself again and again. Don't give an inch until the final buzzer sounds.

—Larry Bird

I learned early on to never walk while I was on the ball field. I ran everywhere I went.

—Enos Slaughter

There are only two options regarding commitment. You're either IN or you're OUT. There is no such thing as life in-between.

—Pat Riley

Some people say I have attitude—maybe I do . . . but I think you have to. You have to believe in yourself when no one else does—that makes you a winner right there.

—Venus Williams

In great attempts it is glorious even to fail.

—Vince Lombardi

Most people give up just when they're about to achieve success. They quit on the one yard line. They give up at the last minute of the game one foot from a winning touchdown.

—Ross Perot

In high school, in sport, I had a coach who told me I was much better than I thought I was, and would make me do more in a positive sense. He was the first person who taught me not to be afraid of failure.

—Mike Krzyzewski

In theory, theory and practice are the same. In practice, they are not.

—Yogi Berra

You have to be able to center yourself, to let all of your emotions go. Don't ever forget that you play with your soul as well as your body.

—Kareem Abdul-Jabbar

Success is never permanent, and failure is never final.

—Mike Ditka

I've had enough success for two lifetimes. My success is talent put together with hard work and luck.

—Kareem Abdul-Jabbar

In order to excel, you must be completely dedicated to your chosen sport. You must also be prepared to work hard and be willing to accept constructive criticism. Without 100 percent dedication, you won't be able to do this.

—Willie Mays

The man who has no imagination has no wings.

—Muhammad Ali

The trick is growing up without growing old.

—Casey Stengel

Make sure your worst enemy doesn't live between your own two ears.

—Laird Hamilton

Sometimes, big trees grow out of acorns. I think I heard that from a squirrel.

—Jerry Coleman

I have observed that baseball is not unlike war, and when you get right down to it, we batters are the heavy artillery.

—Ty Cobb

Demand excellence.

—Emmitt Smith

Set your goals high, and don't stop till you get there.

—Bo Jackson

There are many who lust for the simple answers of doctrine or decree. They are on the left and right. They are not confined to a single part of the society. They are terrorists of the mind.

—A. Bartlett Giamatti

The reason the Mets have played so well at Shea [Stadium] this year is they have the best home record in baseball.

—Ralph Kiner

If you don't have confidence, you'll always find a way not to win.

—Carl Lewis

Just play. Have fun. Enjoy the game.

—Michael Jordan

It's not the size of the dog in the fight, but the size of the fight in the dog!

—Archie Griffin

You can't win unless you learn how to lose.

—Kareem Abdul-Jabbar

Forget your opponents; always play against par.

—Sam Snead

The Spirit of Sports: The spirit of sports gives each of us who participate an opportunity to be creative. Sports knows no sex, age, race, or religion. Sports gives us all the ability to test ourselves mentally, physically, and emotionally in a way no other aspect of life can. For many of us who struggle with 'fitting in' or our identity—sports gives us our first face of confidence. That first bit of confidence can be a gateway to many other great things!

—Dan O'Brien

I always felt that my greatest asset was not my physical ability; it was my mental ability.

—Bruce Jenner

You have to expect things of yourself before you can do them.

—Michael Jordan

You were not born a winner, and you were not born a loser. You are what you make yourself be.

—Lou Holtz

I don't know any other way to lead but by example.

—Don Shula

Talent is God-given. Be humble. Fame is man-given.
Be grateful. Conceit is self-given. Be careful.

—John Wooden

Excellence is not a singular act but a habit. You are
what you do repeatedly.

—Shaquille O'Neal

The superior man blames himself. The inferior man blames others.

—Don Shula

The time when there is no one there to feel sorry for you or to cheer for you is when a player is made.

—Tim Duncan

Never give up! Failure and rejection are only the first step to succeeding.

—Jim Valvano

It's not the disability that defines you; it's how you deal with the challenges the disability presents you with. We have an obligation to the abilities we DO have, not the disability.

—Jim Abbott

Success is not forever and failure isn't fatal.

—Don Shula

It's not what you achieve, it's what you overcome. That's what defines your career.

—Carlton Fisk

330

Confidence on the Field

I think everyone should experience defeat at least once during their career. You learn a lot from it.

—Lou Holtz

Keep away from people who try to belittle your ambitions. Small people always do that, but the really great make you feel that you, too, can become great.

—Lou Holtz

I'm playing; I'm here. I'm going to fight until they tell me they don't want me anymore.

—Steve Nash

331

Don't measure yourself by what you have accomplished, but by what you should have accomplished with your ability.

—John Wooden

Just believe in yourself. Even if you don't, pretend that you do and, at some point, you will.

—Venus Williams

For me, winning isn't something that happens suddenly on the field when the whistle blows and the crowds roar. Winning is something that builds physically and mentally every day that you train and every night that you dream.

—Emmitt Smith

Vision gets the dreams started. Dreaming employs your God-given imagination to reinforce the vision. Both are part of something I believe is absolutely necessary to building the life of a champion, a winner, a person of high character who is consistently at the top of whatever game he or she is in.

—Emmitt Smith

Yesterday's home runs don't win today's games.

—Babe Ruth

Do not let what you cannot do interfere with what you can do.

—John Wooden

Dreaming means 'rehearsing' what you see, playing it over and over in your mind until it becomes as real to you as your life right now.

—Emmitt Smith

The only place success comes before work is in the dictionary.

—Vince Lombardi

10

MISCELLANY

Most folks are about as happy as they make up their minds to be.

—Abraham Lincoln

If you really put a small value upon yourself, rest assured that the world will not raise your price.

—Unknown

Believe in your flyness, conquer your shyness.

—Kanye West

People are crying up the rich and variegated plumage of the peacock, and he is himself blushing at the sight of his ugly feet.

—Sa'Di

Every deep thinker is more afraid of being understood than of being misunderstood.

—Friedrich Nietzsche

People will stare. Make it worth their while.

—Harry Winston

Somewhere, something incredible is waiting to be known.

—Carl Sagan

Miscellany

The world is full of magical things patiently waiting
for our wits to grow sharper.

—Bertrand Russell

One man's observation is another man's closed
book or flight of fancy.

—Willard van Orman Quine

It's in how you carry yourself. I've always been a
very mature person, and I've always known what I
wanted. And I go after it no matter what.

—Aaliyah

The ego is willing but the machine cannot go on. It's the last thing a man will admit, that his mind ages.

—Will Durant

Of course the heart has it reasons, of which reason knows nothing.

—Blaise Pascal, *Pensées*

If we really love ourselves, everything in our life works.

—Louise L. Hay

I know the best moments can never be captured on film, even as I spend nearly half my life trying to do just that.

—Rosie O'Donnell

There is overwhelming evidence that the higher the level of self-esteem, the more likely one will be to treat others with respect, kindness, and generosity.

—Nathaniel Branden

Only the gentle are ever really strong.

—James Dean

The most talented people are always the nicest.

—James Caan

Everybody is ignorant, only on different subjects.

—Will Smith

There is no end. There is no beginning. There is only the infinite passion of life.

—Federico Fellini

To say nothing, especially when speaking, is half the art of diplomacy.

—Will Durant

My hobbies just sort of gradually became my vocation.

—Weird Al Yankovic

I can be changed by what happens to me, but I refuse to be reduced by it.

—Maya Angelou

345

Honesty isn't enough for me. That becomes very boring. If you can convince people what you're doing is real and it's also bigger than life—that's exciting.

—Gene Hackman

I have always tried to be true to myself, to pick those battles I felt were important. My ultimate responsibility is to myself. I could never be anything else.

—Arthur Ashe

Too many people overvalue what they are not and undervalue what they are.

—Malcolm Forbes

Miscellany

Find in yourself those human things which are
universal.

—Sanford Meisner

I think your self emerges more clearly over time.

—Meryl Streep

The courage to be is the courage to accept oneself,
in spite of being unacceptable.

—Paul Tillich

But the real secret to total gorgeousness is to believe in yourself, have self-confidence, and try to be secure in your decisions and thoughts.

—Kirsten Dunst

They can't scare me, if I scare them first.

—Lady Gaga

Never be bullied into silence. Never allow yourself to be made a victim. Accept no one's definition of your life, but define yourself.

—Harvey Fierstein

Beauty is grace and confidence. I've learned to accept and appreciate what nature gave me.

—Lindsay Lohan

The good ideas will survive.

—Quentin Tarantino

Confidence is preparation. Everything else is beyond your control.

—Richard Kline

By nature, I keep moving, man. My theory is, be the shark. You've just got to keep moving. You can't stop.

—Brad Pitt

Things do not happen. Things are made to happen.

—John F. Kennedy

I always say don't make plans, make options.

—Jennifer Aniston

Success comes in cans, not cant's.

—Unknown

This is really a lovely horse, I once rode her mother.

—Ted Walsh

A good head and a good heart are always a formidable combination.

—Nelson Mandela

The enemy of art is the absence of limitations.

—Orson Welles

Self-confidence is the best outfit. Rock it and own it.

—Unknown

I have a different vision of leadership. A leader is someone who brings people together.

—George W. Bush

Tact is the ability to tell someone to go to hell in such a way that they look forward to the trip.

—Winston Churchill

It's impossible, said pride. It's risky, said experience. It's pointless, said reason. Give it a try, whispered the heart.

—Unknown

Ask not what your country can do for you; ask what you can do for your country.

—John F. Kennedy

We have to learn to be our own best friends because we fall too easily into the trap of being our own worst enemies.

—Roderick Thorp, *Rainbow Drive*

If you can't convince them, confuse them.

—Harry S. Truman

A wizard is never late, nor is he early; he arrives precisely when he means to.

—Peter Jackson

Whatever you are, be a good one.

—Abraham Lincoln

Whoever is happy will make others happy, too.

—Mark Twain

You are ambitious, which, within reasonable
bounds, does good rather than harm.

—Abraham Lincoln

Be so good they can't ignore you.

—Steve Martin

Never trust a man who has no vices.

—Winston Churchill

I think happiness is what makes you pretty. Period. Happy people are beautiful. They become like a mirror and they reflect that happiness.

—Drew Barrymore

There comes a time when silence is betrayal.

—Martin Luther King Jr.

Always bear in mind that your own resolution to succeed is more important than any other.

—Abraham Lincoln

You teach people how to treat you by what you allow, what you stop, and what you reinforce.

—Tony Gaskins

357

We must not measure greatness from the mansion down, but from the manger up.

—Jesse Jackson

What counts is not necessarily the size of the dog in the fight, it's the size of the fight in the dog.

—Dwight D. Eisenhower

Indecision may or may not be my problem.

—Jimmy Buffett

Miscellany

No matter how many times you tell a girl she is beautiful, she will never believe you if she doesn't believe in herself.

—Katherine Beaulieu

Drama is life with the dull bits cut out.

—Alfred Hitchcock

The only kind of dignity which is genuine is that which is not diminished by the indifference of others.

—Dag Hammarskjöld

Confidence . . . thrives on honesty, on honor, on the sacredness of obligations, on faithful protection, and on unselfish performance. Without them it cannot live.

—Franklin D. Roosevelt

Your value doesn't decrease based on someone's inability to see your worth.

—Unknown

When I take action, I'm not going to fire a $2 million missile at a $10 empty tent and hit a camel in the butt. It's going to be decisive.

—George W. Bush

Miscellany

I'm confident because I have a camel in my tent.

—Rene

Just keep moving forward and don't give a shit about what anybody thinks. Do what you have to do, for you.

—Johnny Depp

It ain't what they call you; it's what you answer to.

—W. C. Fields

Audiences deserve better.

—Leonard Maltin

A successful person is one who can lay a firm foundation with the bricks that others throw at him or her.

—David Brinkley

One feels the excitement of hearing an untold story.

—John Hope

Miscellany

We all have our limitations, but when we listen to our critics, we also have theirs.

—Robert Brault

The chief incalculable in war is the human will.

—B. H. Liddell Hart

Why worry? If you've done the very best you can, worrying won't make it any better.

—Walt Disney

I am not bound to succeed, but I am bound to live up to what light I have.

—Abraham Lincoln

People demand freedom of speech as a compensation for the freedom of thought which they seldom use.

—Søren Kierkegaard

My assumption is that fundamentally the picture of the human animal, as developed by Freud, is largely right.

—Peter Gay

Don't compromise yourself. You're all you've got.

—Janis Joplin

To free us from the expectations of others, to give us back to ourselves—there lies the great, the singular power of self-respect.

—Joan Didion, *Slouching Towards Bethlehem*

Just as much as we see in others we have in ourselves.

—William Hazlitt

Believe in yourself and there will come a day when others will have no choice but to believe with you.

—Cynthia Kersey

Compliment people. Magnify their strengths, not their weaknesses.

—Unknown

If I'm not complaining, I'm not having a good time.

—Martin Scorsese

Miscellany

Anxiety is the handmaiden of creativity.

—Chuck Jones

Those who are truly comfortable with themselves
and their achievements take pleasure in being who
they are . . . they don't need to tell the world about it.

—Nathaniel Branden

As filmmakers, we can show where a person's
mind goes, as opposed to theater, which is more to
sit back and watch it.

—Darren Aronofsky

Our remedies oft in ourselves do lie / Which we ascribe to heaven.

—William Shakespeare, *All's Well That Ends Well*

The man who acquires the ability to take full possession of his own mind may take possession of anything else to which he is justly entitled.

—Andrew Carnegie, "The Gospel of Wealth," from the *North American Review*

The moment you doubt whether you can fly, you cease forever to be able to do it.

—J. M. Barrie, *Peter Pan*

Miscellany

Surround yourself with the right people, and realize your own worth. Honestly, there are enough bad people out there in the world—you don't need to be your own worst enemy.

—Lucy Hale

I have been and still am a seeker, but I have ceased to question stars and books; I have begun to listen to the teaching my blood whispers to me.

—Hermann Hesse, *Demian*

Your self-worth is determined by you. You don't have to depend on someone telling you who you are.

—Beyoncé Knowles

You are here to enable the divine purpose of the universe to unfold. That is how important you are!

—Eckhart Tolle, *The Power of Now*

To love yourself right now, just as you are, is to give yourself heaven. Don't wait until you die. If you wait, you die now. If you love, you live now.

—Alan Cohen

Right now I have more confidence in myself. I grew up.

—Amelie Mauresmo

INDEX

1,001 Pearls of Wisdom to Build Confidence

Index

Index

Index

Index

Index

Index

385

1,001 Pearls of Wisdom to Build Confidence

Index